HAL•LEONARD®

GUITAR PLAY-ALONG

AUDIO
ACCESS
INCLUDED

PLAYBACK+
Speed • Pitch • Balance • Loop

 VOL

METALLICA

1991 - 2

Play 8 Songs with Tab and Sound-alike Audio

Cover photo © Getty Images / Frank Micelotta

To access audio visit:
www.halleonard.com/mylibrary

Enter Code
4883-2874-0793-1716

ISBN 978-1-4950-9480-4

Visit Hal Leonard Online at
www.halleonard.com

Contact Us:
Hal Leonard
7777 West Bluemound Road
Milwaukee, WI 53213
Email: info@halleonard.com

In Europe contact:
Hal Leonard Europe Limited
Distribution Centre, Newmarket Road
Bury St Edmunds, Suffolk, IP33 3YB
Email: info@halleonardeurope.com

In Australia contact:
Hal Leonard Australia Pty. Ltd.
4 Lentara Court
Cheltenham, Victoria, 3192 Australi
Email: info@halleonard.com.au

C000130123

GUITAR NOTATION LEGEND

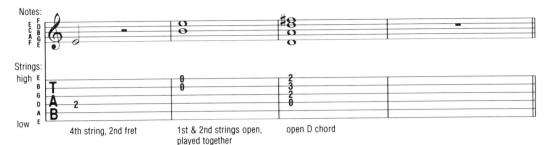

THE MUSICAL STAFF shows pitches and rhythms and is divided by bar lines into measures. Pitches are named after the first seven letters of the alphabet.

TABLATURE graphically represents the guitar fingerboard. Each horizontal line represents a string, and each number represents a fret.

4th string, 2nd fret

1st & 2nd strings open, played together

open D chord

HALF-STEP BEND: Strike the note and bend up 1/2 step.

WHOLE-STEP BEND: Strike the note and bend up one step.

GRACE NOTE BEND: Strike the note and immediately bend up as indicated.

SLIGHT (MICROTONE) BEND: Strike the note and bend up 1/4 step.

BEND AND RELEASE: Strike the note and bend up as indicated, then release back to the original note. Only the first note is struck.

PRE-BEND: Bend the note as indicated, then strike it.

VIBRATO: The string is vibrated by rapidly bending and releasing the note with the fretting hand.

PALM MUTING: The note is partially muted by the pick hand lightly touching the string(s) just before the bridge.

HAMMER-ON: Strike the first (lower) note with one finger, then sound the higher note (on the same string) with another finger by fretting it without picking.

PULL-OFF: Place both fingers on the notes to be sounded. Strike the first note and without picking, pull the finger off to sound the second (lower) note.

LEGATO SLIDE: Strike the first note and then slide the same fret-hand finger up or down to the second note. The second note is not struck.

SHIFT SLIDE: Same as legato slide, except the second note is struck.

TRILL: Very rapidly alternate between the notes indicated by continuously hammering on and pulling off.

TAPPING: Hammer ("tap") the fret indicated with the pick-hand index or middle finger and pull off to the note fretted by the fret hand.

NATURAL HARMONIC: Strike the note while the fret-hand lightly touches the string directly over the fret indicated.

PINCH HARMONIC: The note is fretted normally and a harmonic is produced by adding the edge of the thumb or the tip of the index finger of the pick hand to the normal pick attack.

TREMOLO PICKING: The note is picked as rapidly and continuously as possible.

VIBRATO BAR DIVE AND RETURN: The pitch of the note or chord is dropped a specified number of steps (in rhythm), then returned to the original pitch.

VIBRATO BAR SCOOP: Depress the bar just before striking the note, then quickly release the bar.

VIBRATO BAR DIP: Strike the note and then immediately drop a specified number of steps, then release back to the original pitch.

Additional Musical Definitions

 (accent) • Accentuate note (play it louder).

 (staccato) • Play the note short.

D.S. al Coda • Go back to the sign ($\%$), then play until the measure marked "*To Coda*," then skip to the section labelled "**Coda**."

D.C. al Fine • Go back to the beginning of the song and play until the measure marked "*Fine*" (end).

Fill • Label used to identify a brief melodic figure which is to be inserted into the arrangement.

N.C. • Harmony is implied.

 • Repeat measures between signs.

 • When a repeated section has different endings, play the first ending only the first time and the second ending only the second time.

CONTENTS

The Day That Never Comes

Music by Metallica
Lyrics by James Hetfield

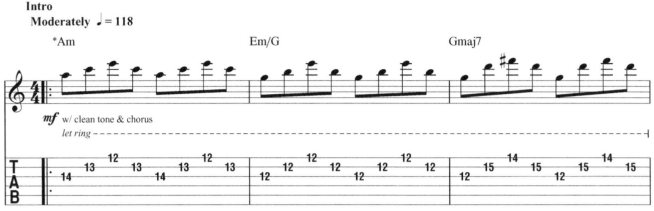

*Chord symbols reflect overall harmony.

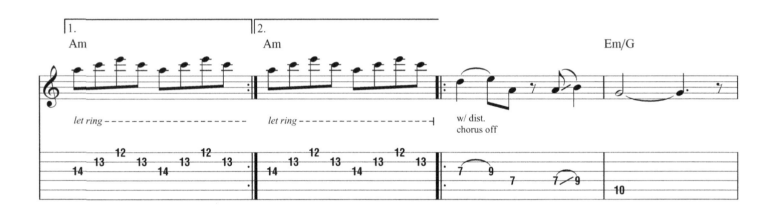

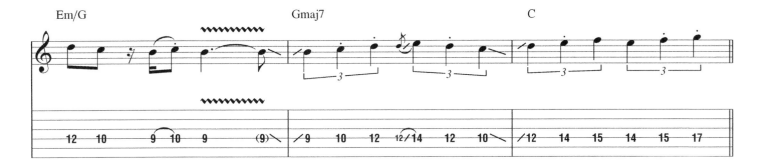

Interlude
Slightly faster ♩ = 120

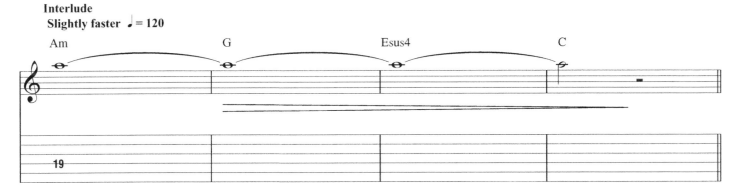

𝄋 **Verse**

2nd time, substitute Fill 1

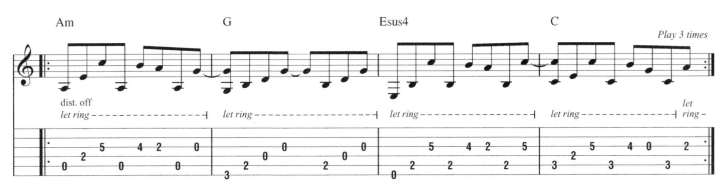

1. Born to push you a - round,
2. *See additional lyrics*

bet-ter just stay down.

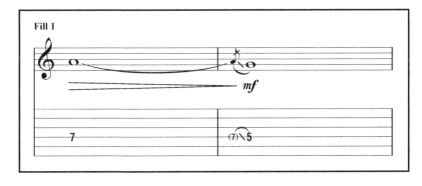

Fill 1

mf

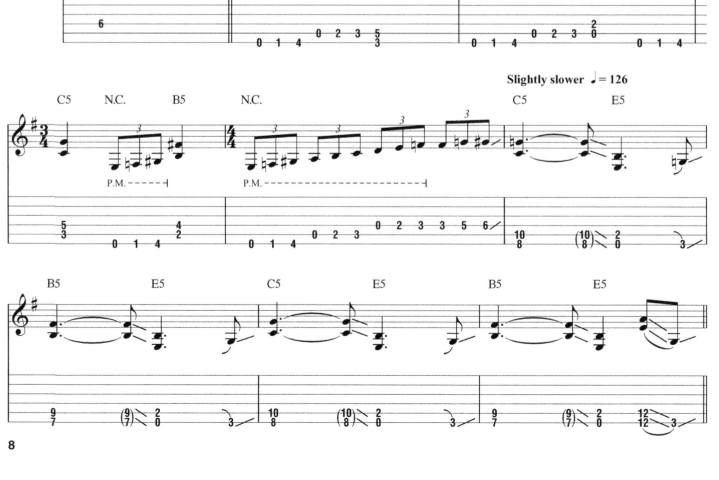

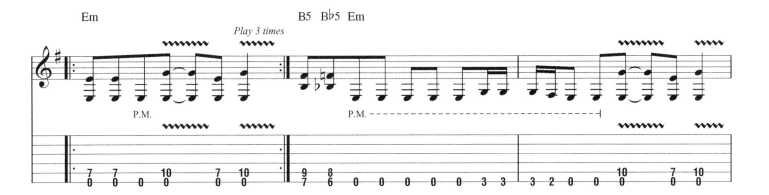

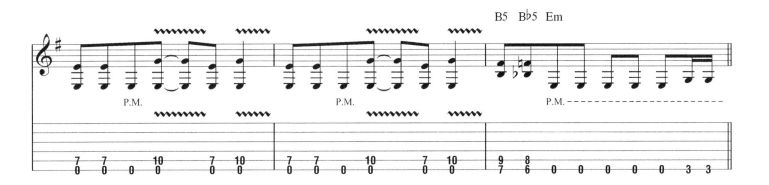

Bridge

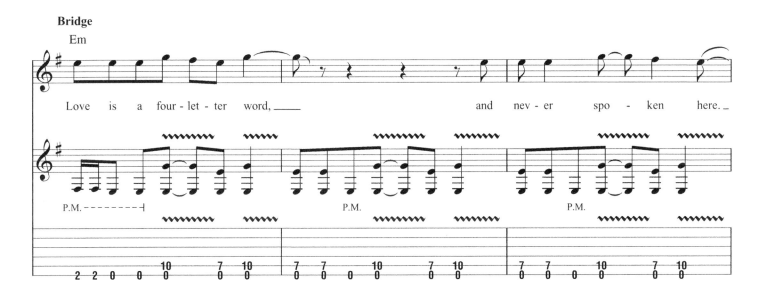

Love is a four-let-ter word, _____ and nev-er spo-ken here. _

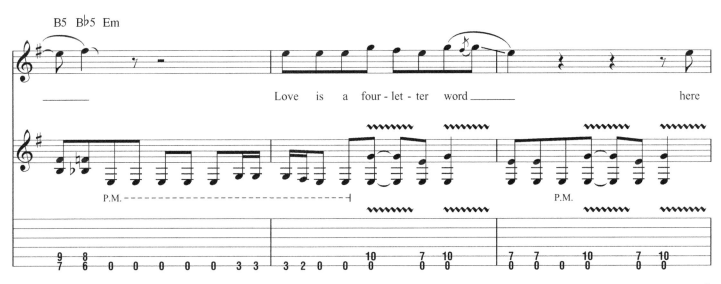

_____ Love is a four-let-ter word _____ here

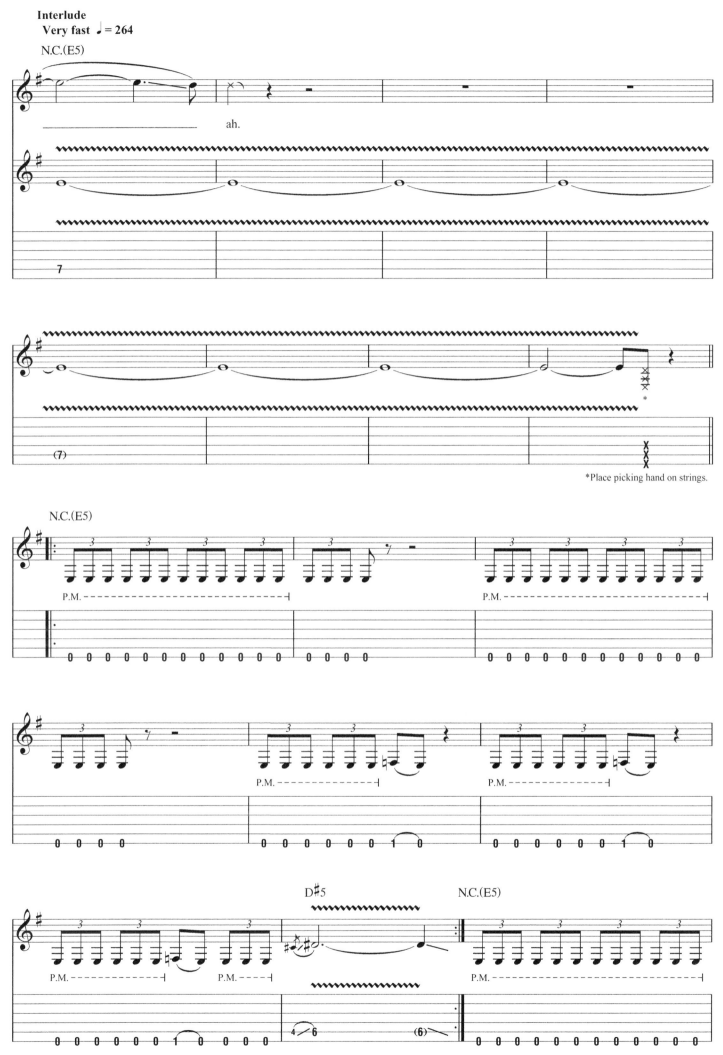

*Place picking hand on strings.

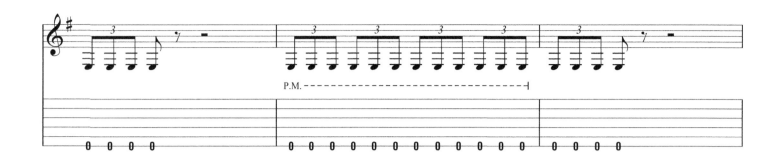

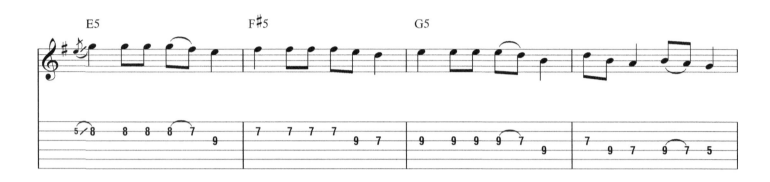

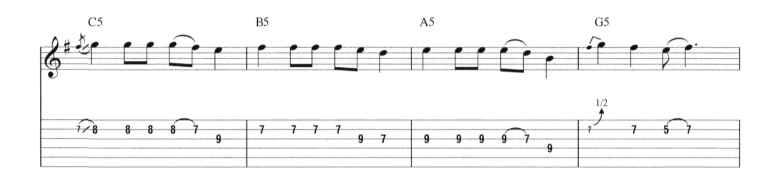

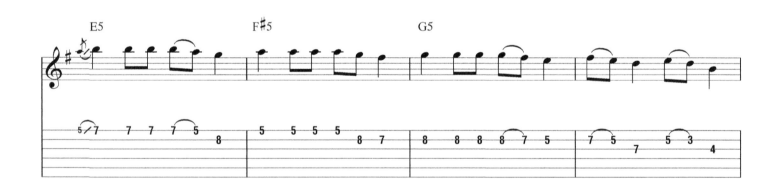

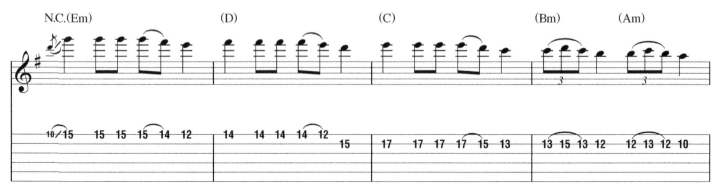

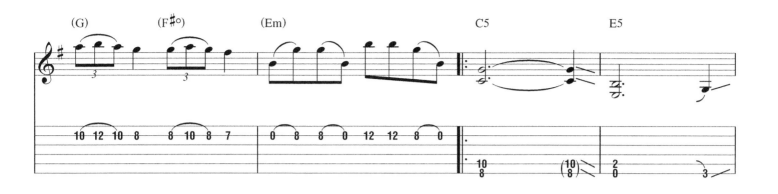

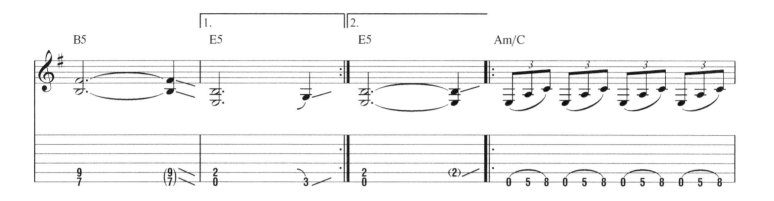

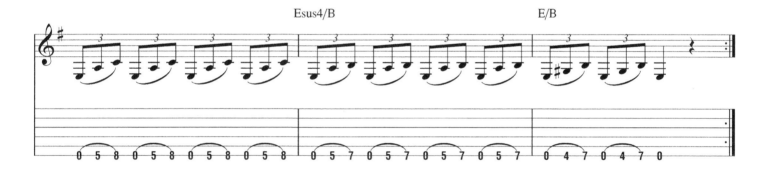

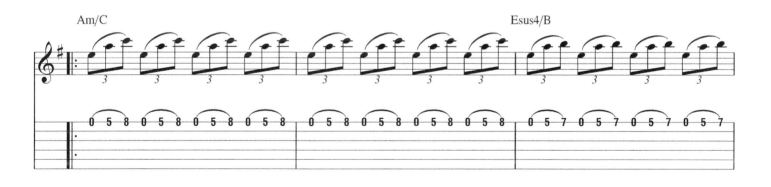

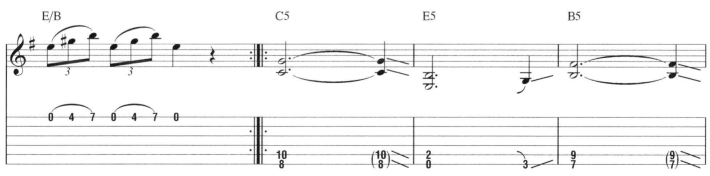

Slightly slower ♩ = 260

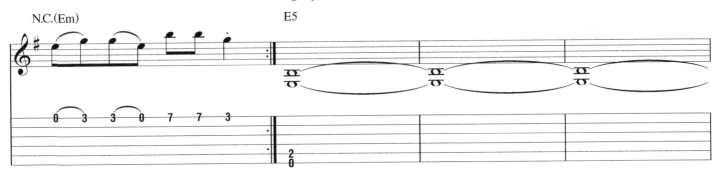

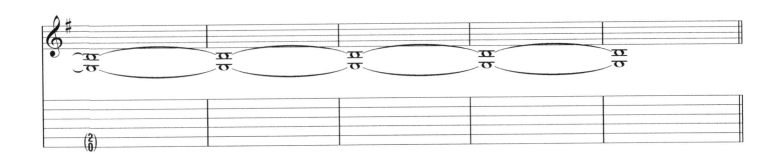

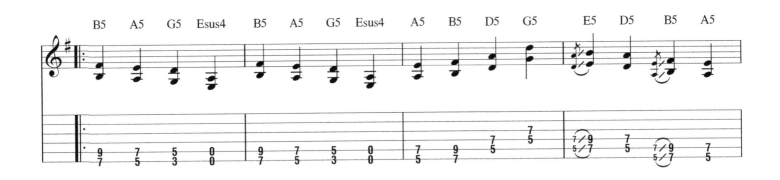

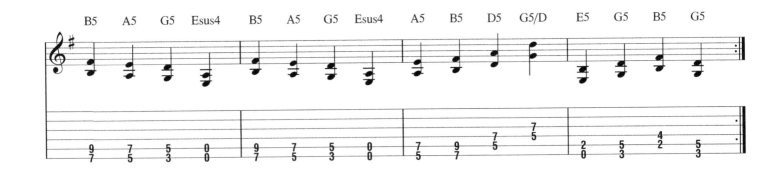

Guitar Solo
Slightly faster ♩ = 268

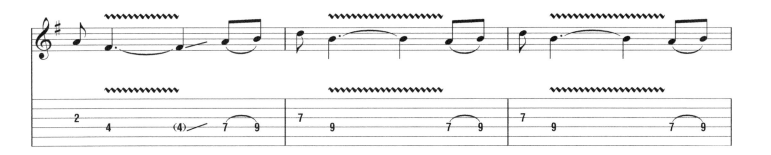

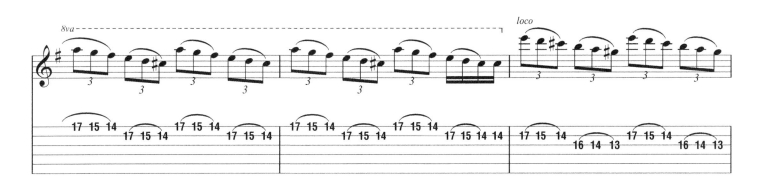

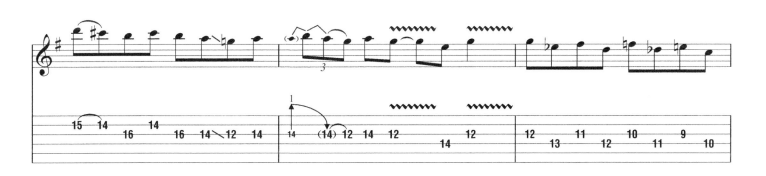

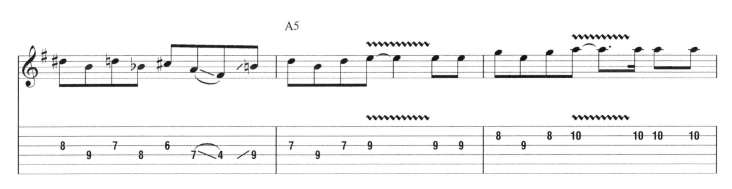

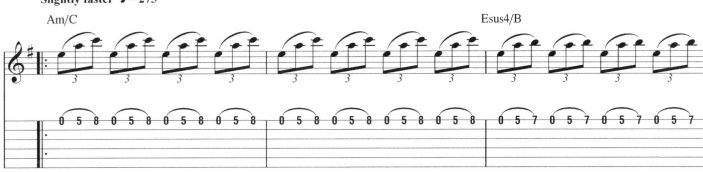

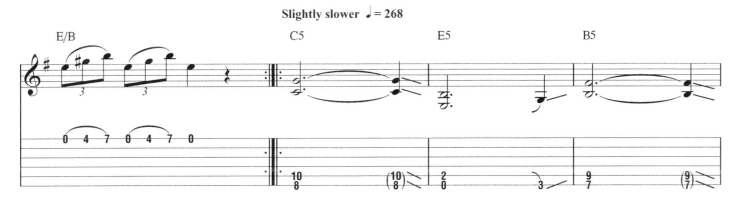

Additional Lyrics

2. Push you 'cross that line; just stay down this time.
   Hide in yourself, crawl in yourself; you'll have your time.
   God, I'll make them pay, ah, take it back one day.
   I'll end this day; I'll splatter color on this gray.

Frantic

Words and Music by James Hetfield, Lars Ulrich, Kirk Hammett and Bob Rock

Drop D tuning, down 1 step:
(low to high) C-G-C-F-A-D

Intro

Moderately fast ♩ = 162

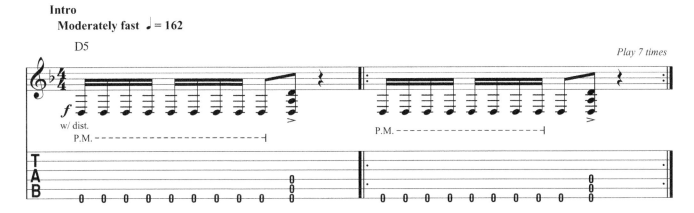

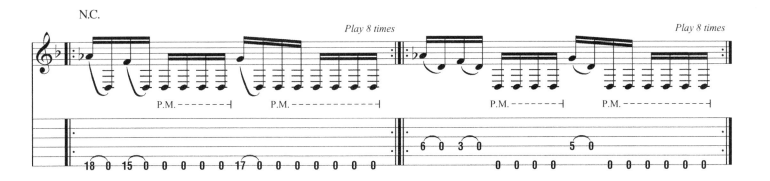

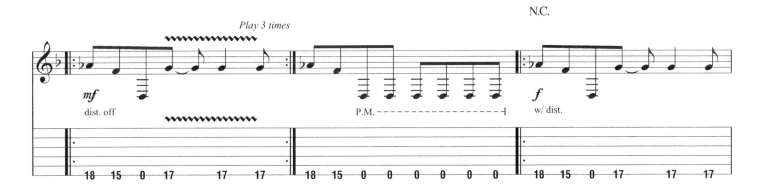

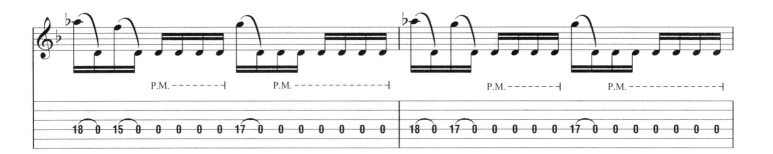

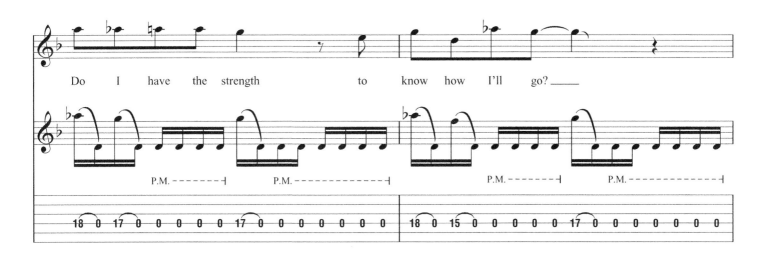

Do I have the strength to know how I'll go? _____

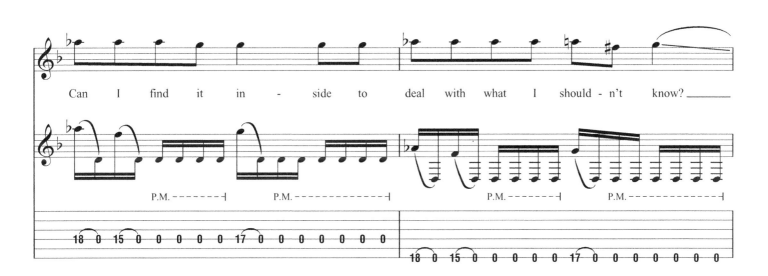

Can I find it in - side to deal with what I should - n't know? _____

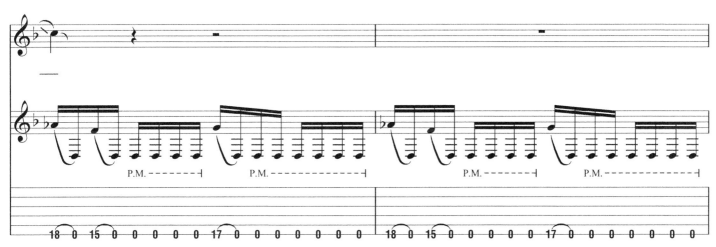

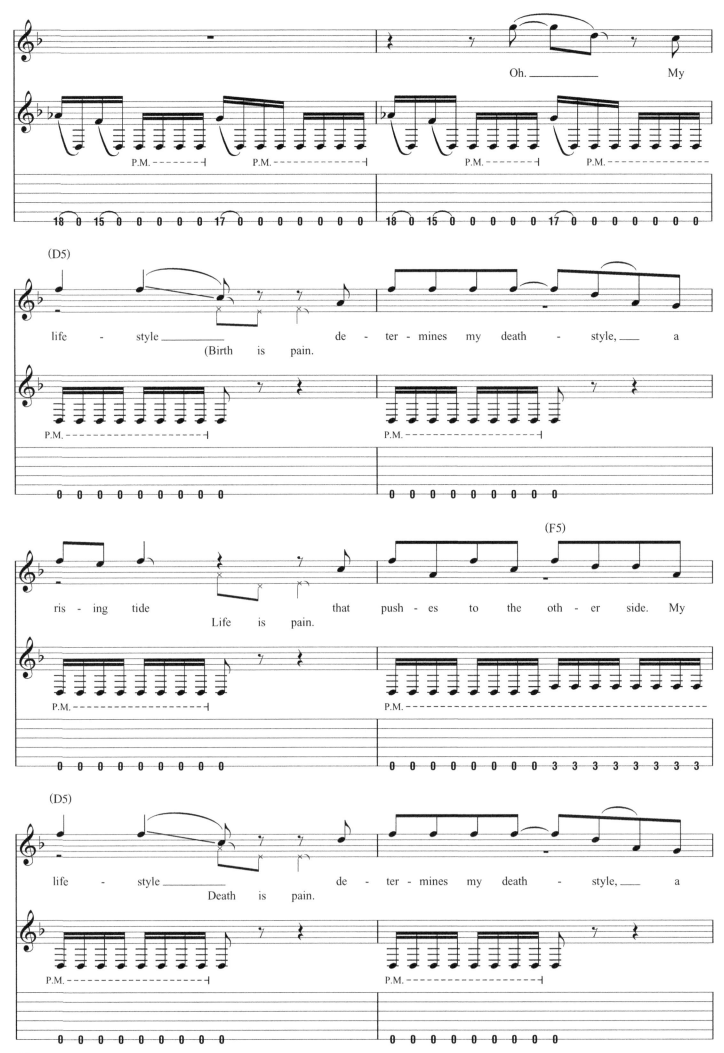

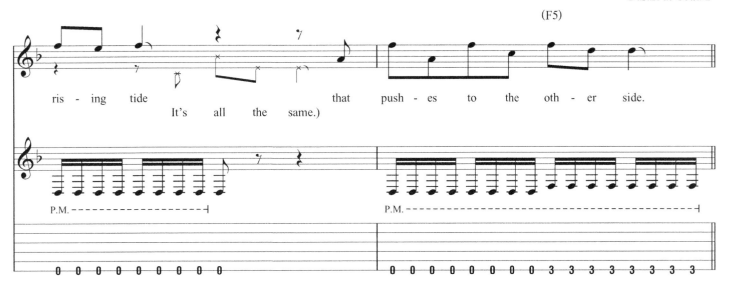

ris - ing tide   that push - es   to   the   oth - er   side.
It's   all   the   same.)

 Coda 2

Outro
Slower ♩ = 122

D5

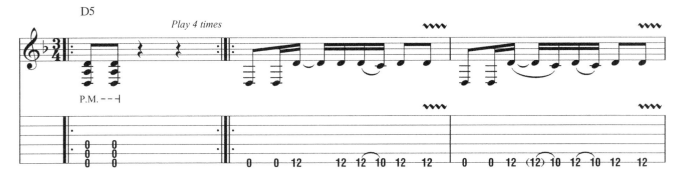

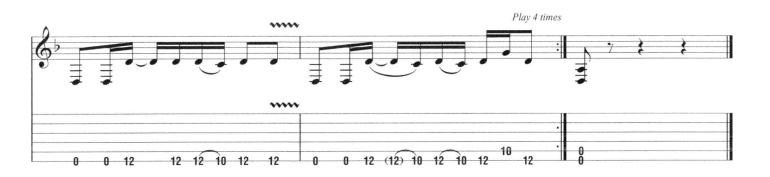

Additional Lyrics

2. I've worn out always being afraid, an endless stream of fear that I've made.
   Treading water full of worry, this frantic, tick, tick, talk of hurry.
   Do I have the strength to know how I'll go?
   Can I find it inside to deal with what I shouldn't know?
   Worn out always being afraid, an endless stream of fear that I've made.

Enter Sandman

Words and Music by James Hetfield, Lars Ulrich and Kirk Hammett

Intro
Moderately ♩ = 123

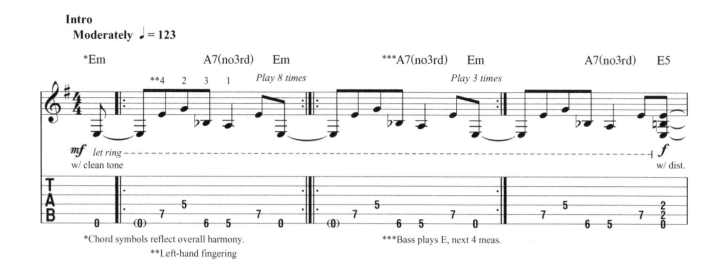

*Chord symbols reflect overall harmony.
**Left-hand fingering

***Bass plays E, next 4 meas.

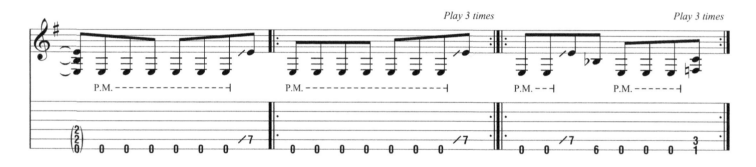

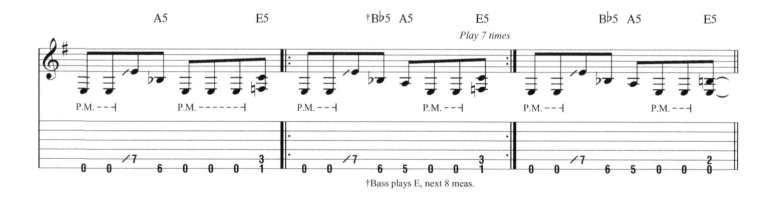

†Bass plays E, next 8 meas.

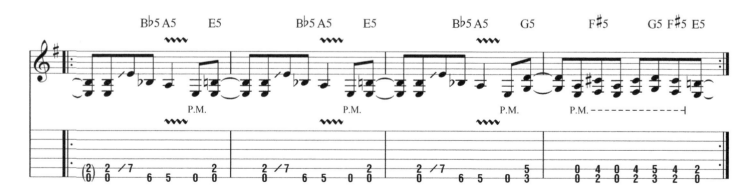

Verse

2. Some-thing's wrong; shut the light. Heav-y thoughts to - night, _____ and they aren't of Snow White. _____

_____ Dreams of war, dreams of liars, dreams of dra-gon's fire, _____

D.S. al Coda

_____ and of things that will bite, _____ yeah.

Coda

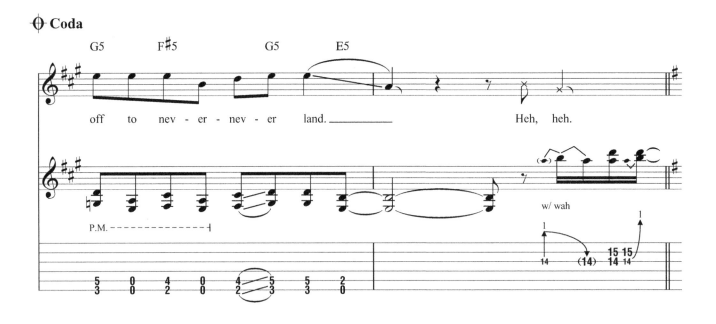

off to nev - er - nev - er land. _____ Heh, heh.

Guitar Solo

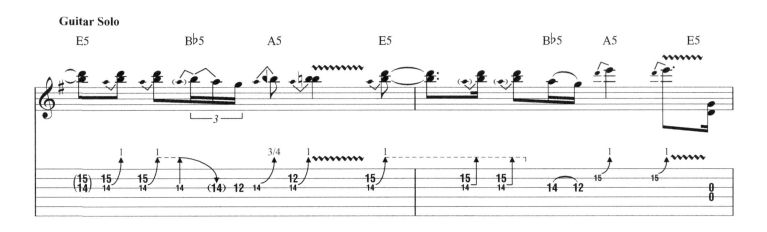

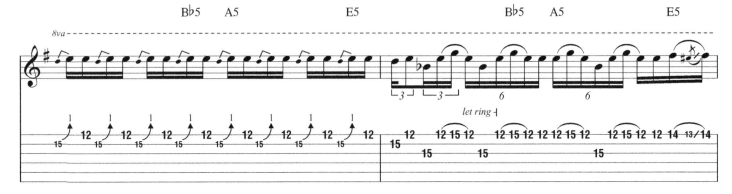

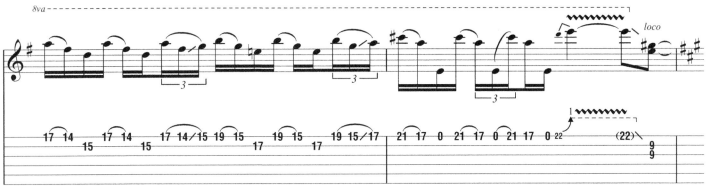

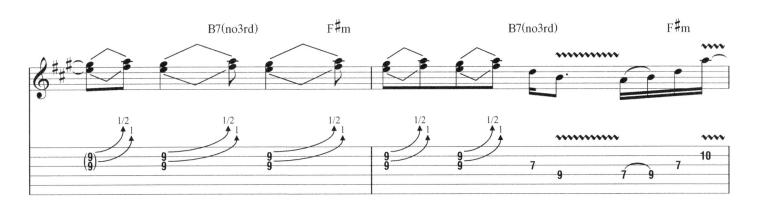

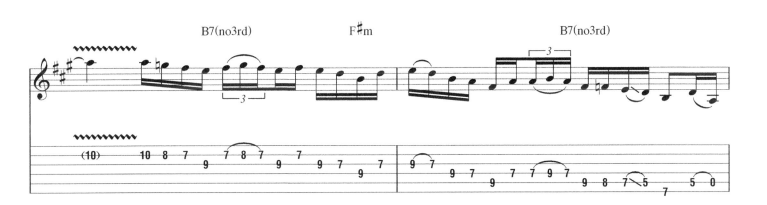

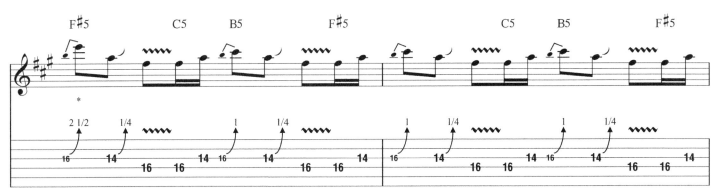

*On original recording, string is bent downward to
 fret edge, hitting 17th fret while bent 2 steps.

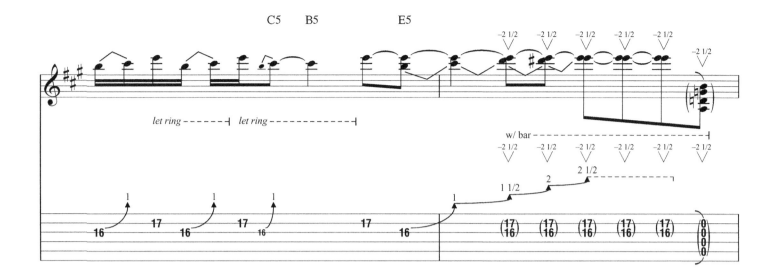

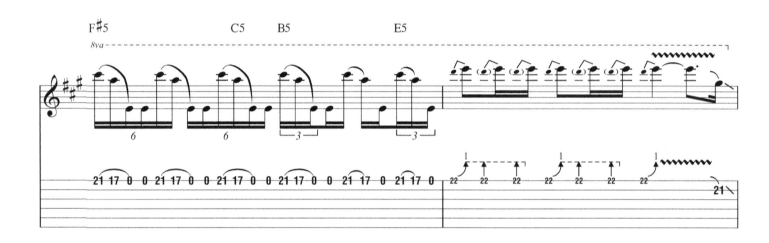

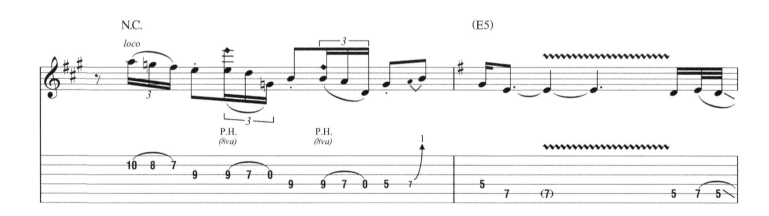

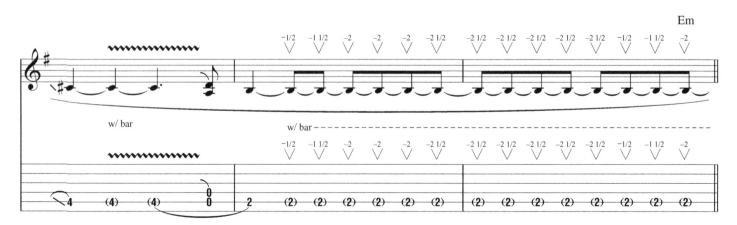

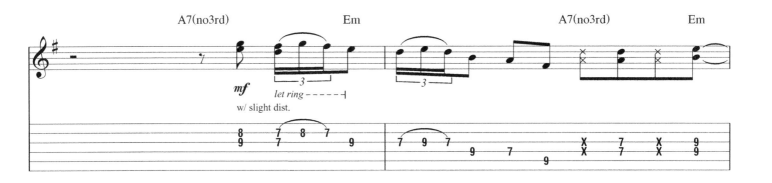

Begin fade

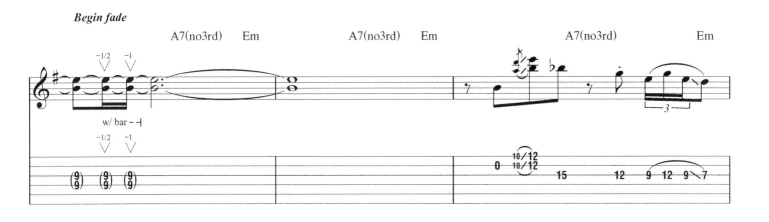

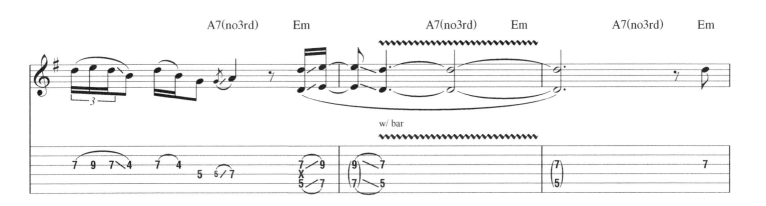

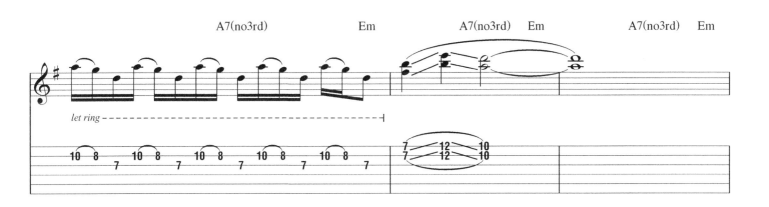

Fade out

Fuel

Words and Music by James Hetfield, Lars Ulrich and Kirk Hammett

Tune down 1/2 step:
(low to high) Eb-Ab-Db-Gb-Bb-Eb

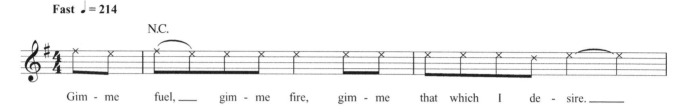

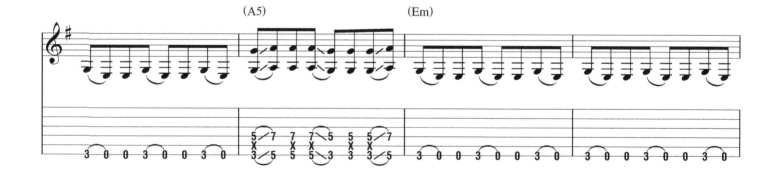

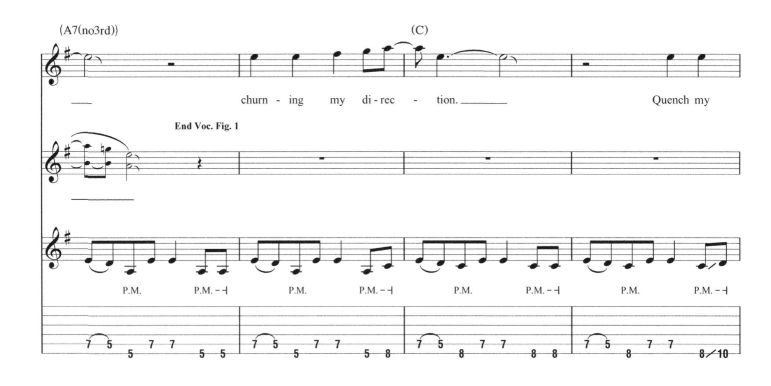

churn-ing my di-rec - tion._____ Quench my

End Voc. Fig. 1

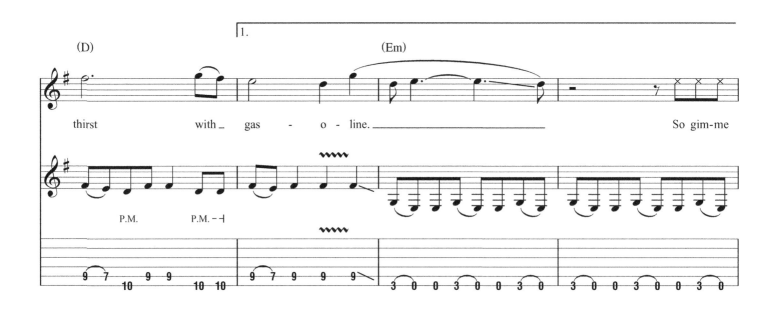

1.

thirst with _ gas - o - line._____ So gim-me

Interlude

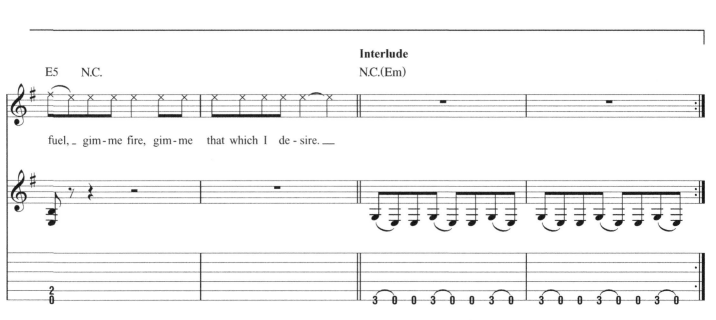

fuel, _ gim-me fire, gim-me that which I de-sire. __

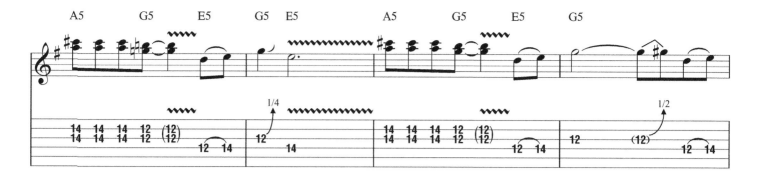

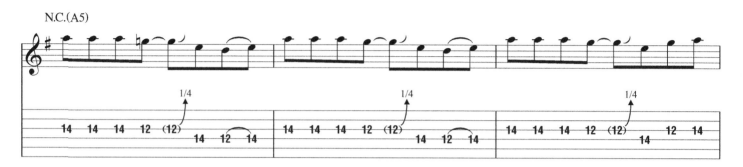

Guitar Solo

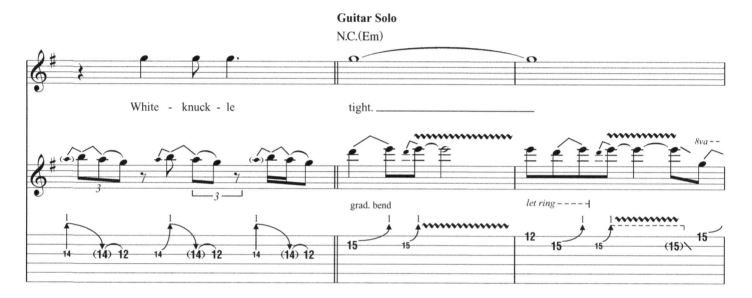

White - knuck - le   tight.

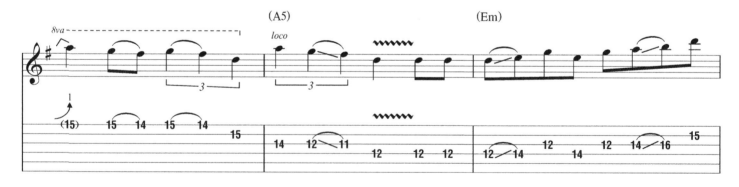

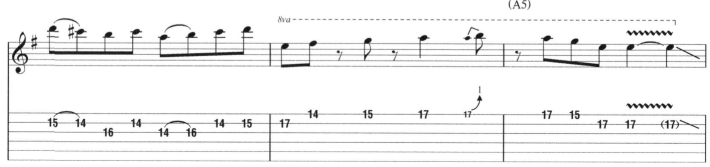

46

Outro

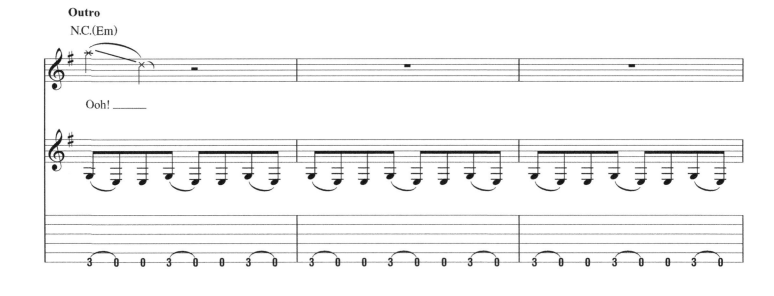

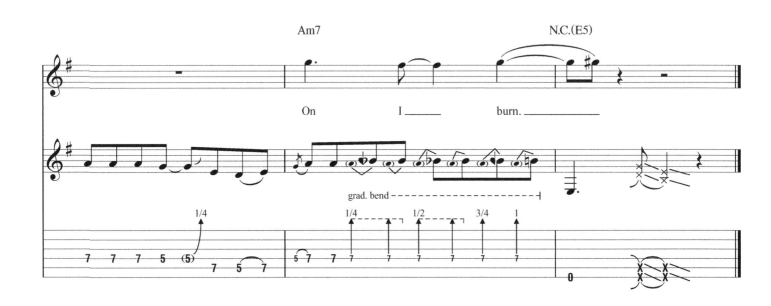

Additional Lyrics

2. Turn on beyond the bone.
   Swallow future, spit out home.
   Burn your face upon the chrome.
   Yeah, oh, yeah.
   Take the corner, join the crash, ah.
   Headlights, (headlines), headlines,
   Another junkie lives too fast.
   Yeah, lives way too fast, (fast), fast, (fast), fast, (fast), whoa.

King Nothing

Words and Music by James Hetfield, Lars Ulrich and Kirk Hammett

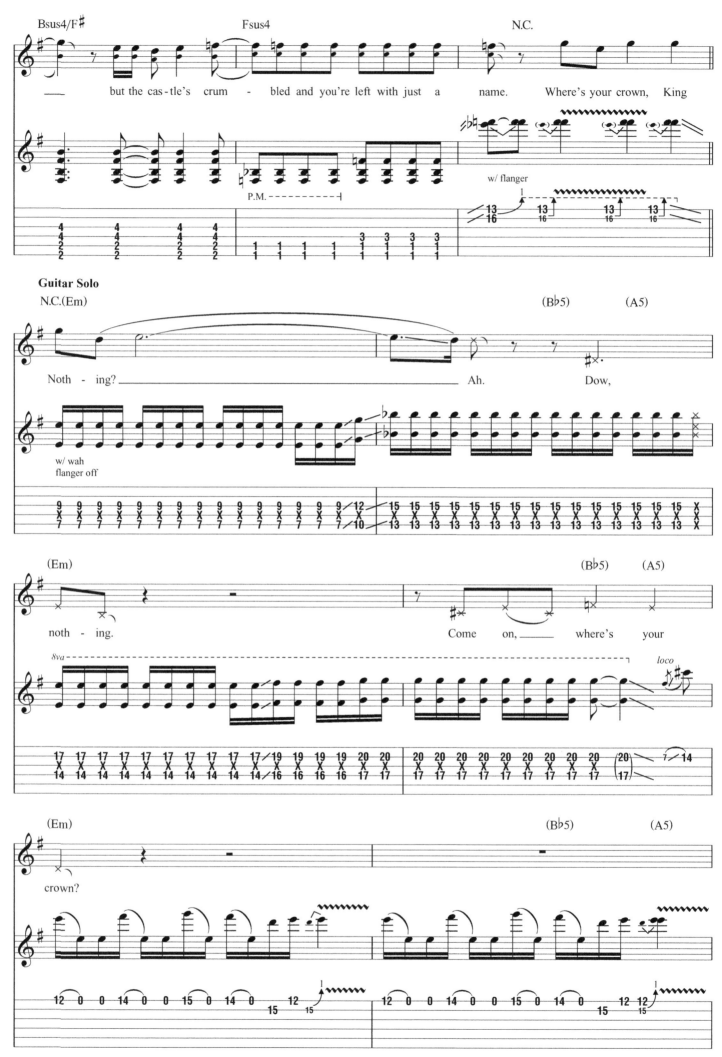

Moth into Flame

Words and Music by James Hetfield and Lars Ulrich

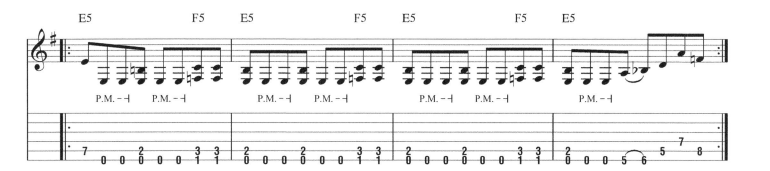

Verse

N.C.(E5)

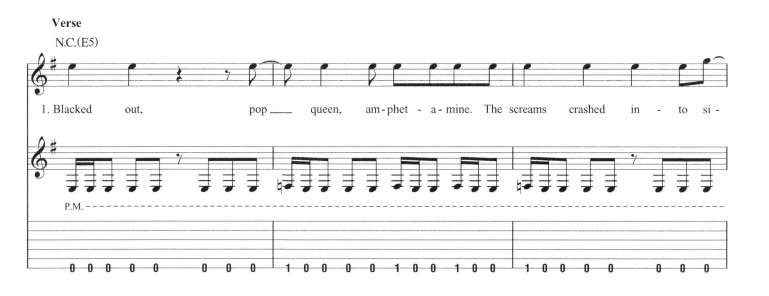

1. Blacked out, pop ___ queen, am-phet - a - mine. The screams crashed in - to si -

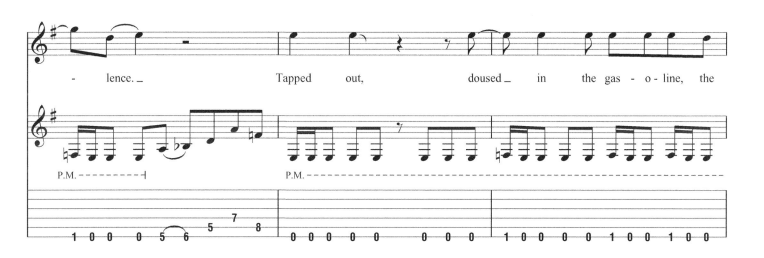

- lence. ___ Tapped out, doused ___ in the gas - o - line, the

high times go - ing time - less. ___ Dec - a - dence, death ___

kill the truth.
tell the truth.
no ex - cuse.

You're fall-ing, but you think you're fly-ing high, high a -

Interlude

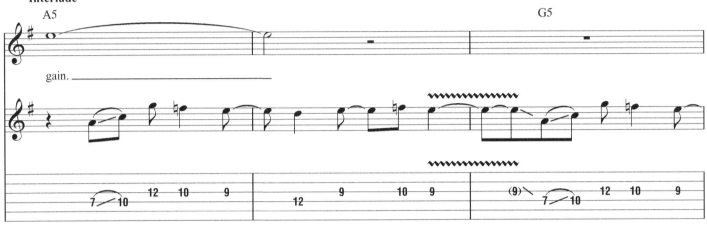

gain.

3rd time, substitute Fill 1

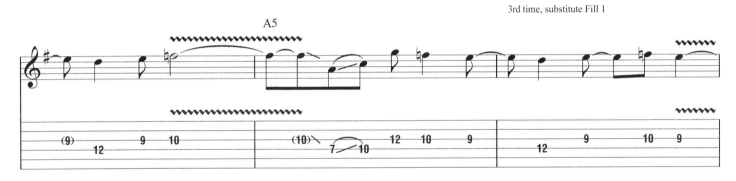

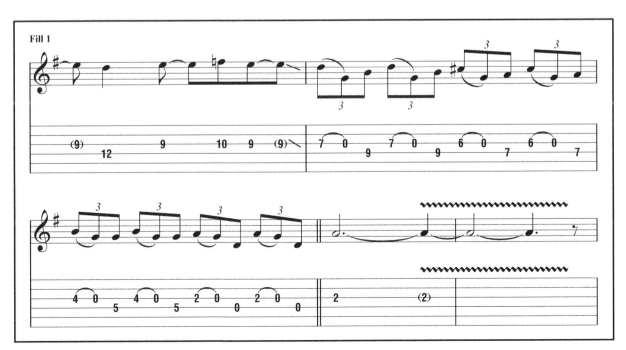

Fill 1

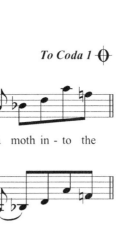

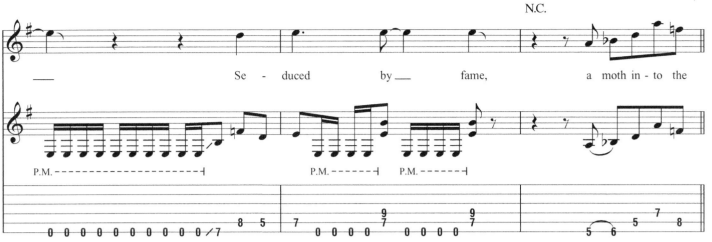

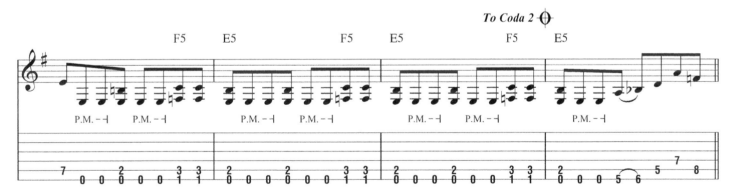

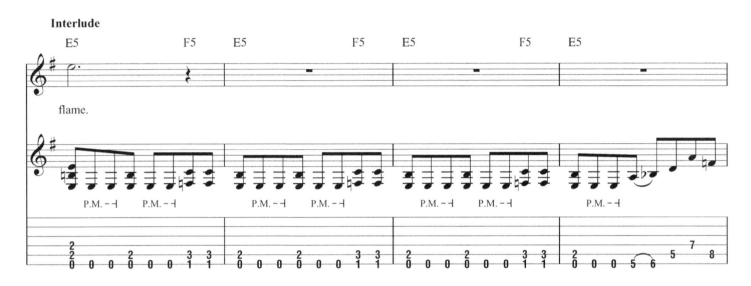

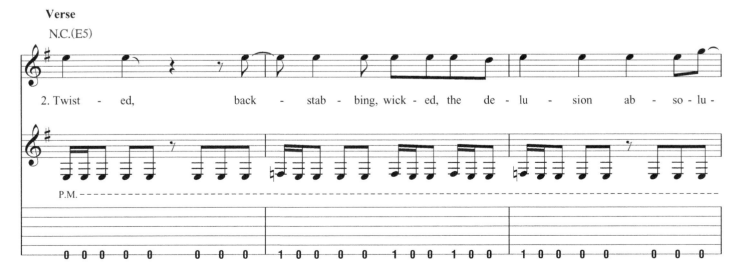

- tion. ____ Per - jur - er, fame ____ is the mur - der - er, se -

D.S. al Coda 1   ⊕ **Coda 1**

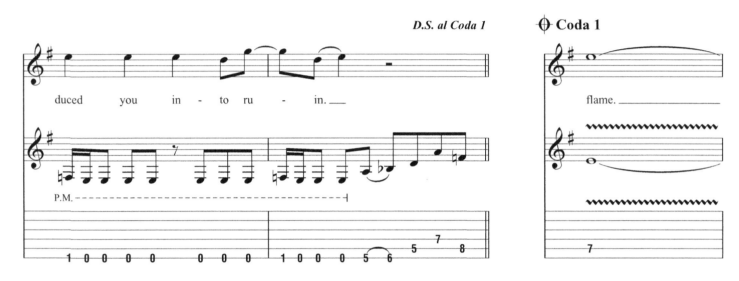

duced you in - to ru - in. ____   flame. ____

Interlude

F5   G5   A5   B♭5   E5   G5   A5

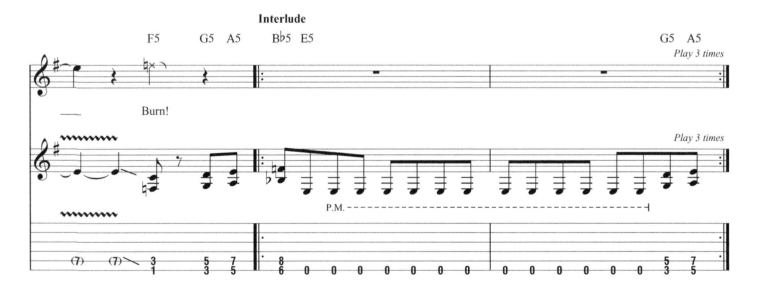

____ Burn!

Play 3 times

B♭5   E5   N.C.(E5)   B♭5   E5

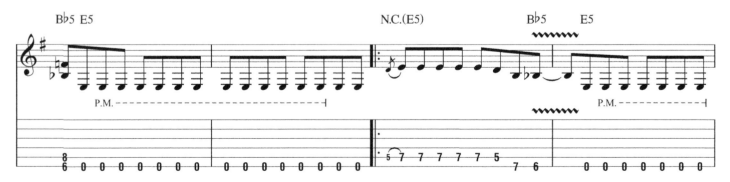

Bridge

Guar - an - tee your name, you go and kill your - self. The vul - tures feast a -

round you still. O - ver - dose on shame and in - se - cur - i - ty. If

Guitar Solo

one won't do, that fist - ful will.

w/ wah

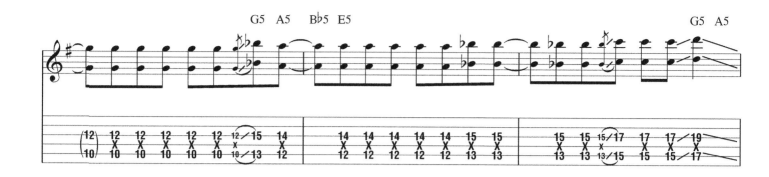

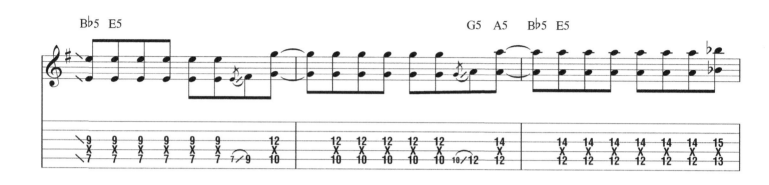

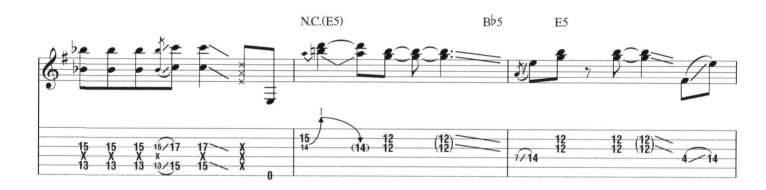

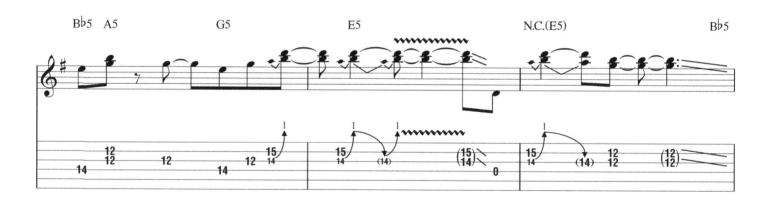

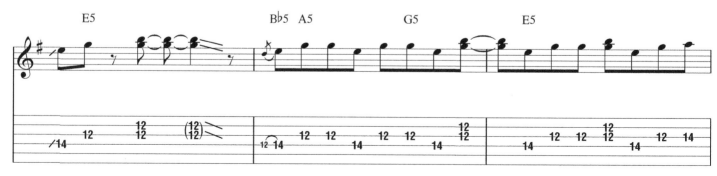

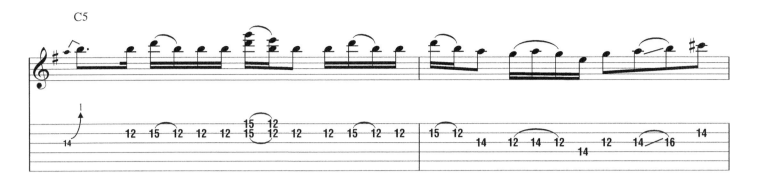

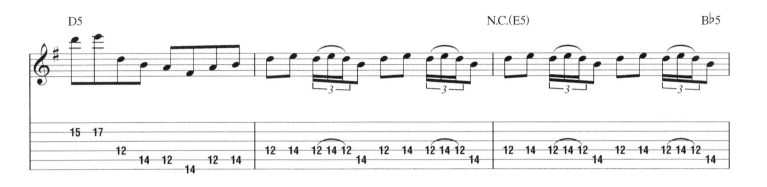

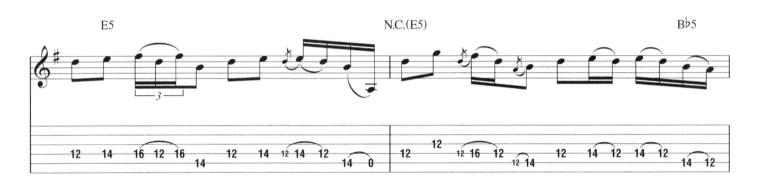

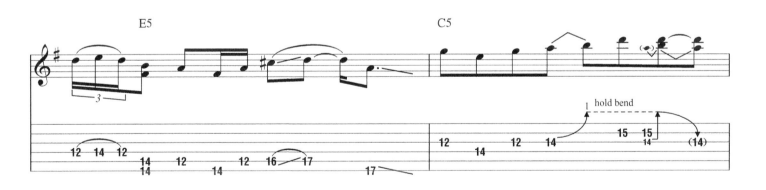

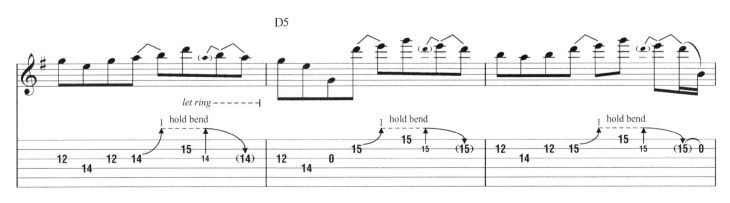

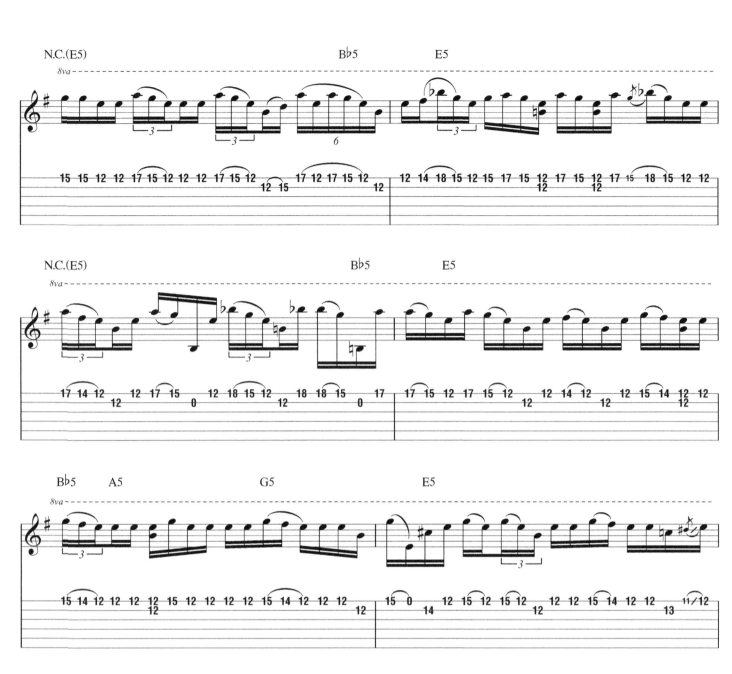
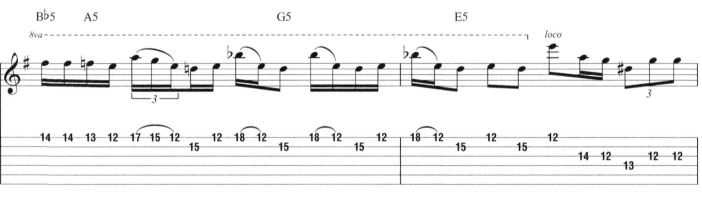
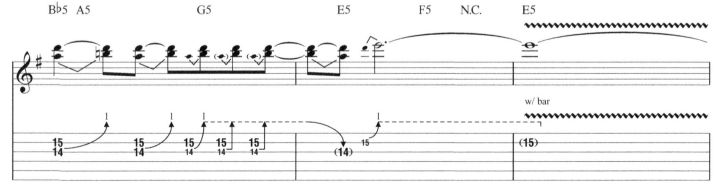

Interlude

Verse

3. Death scene, black hearse, the lim-ou-sine, a grave filled with se-duc-

- tion. Vac-cine, fame does the mur-der-ing. She

Nothing Else Matters

Words and Music by James Hetfield and Lars Ulrich

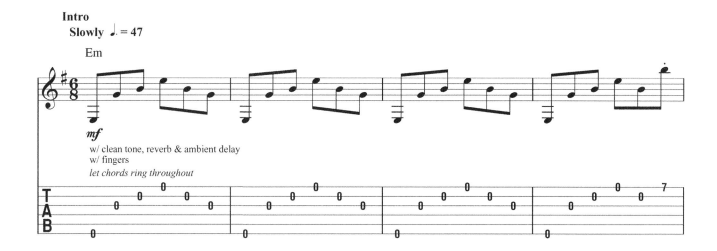

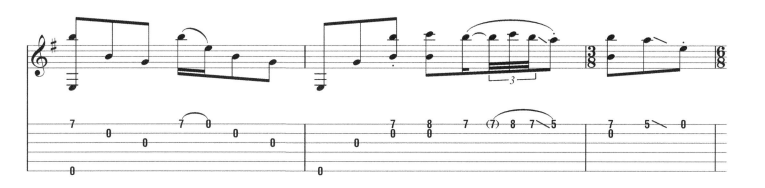

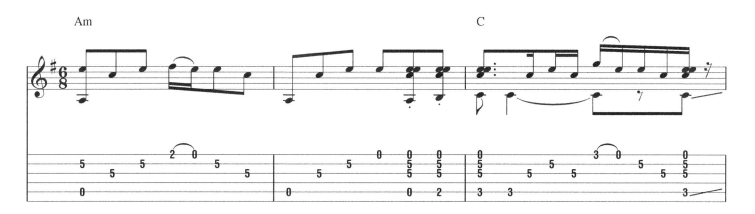

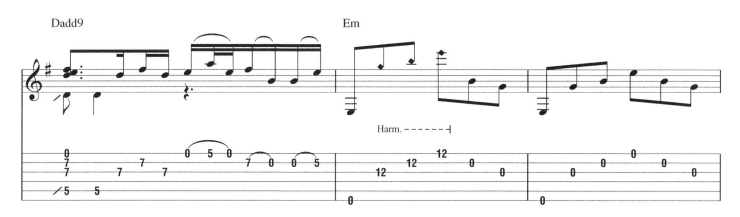

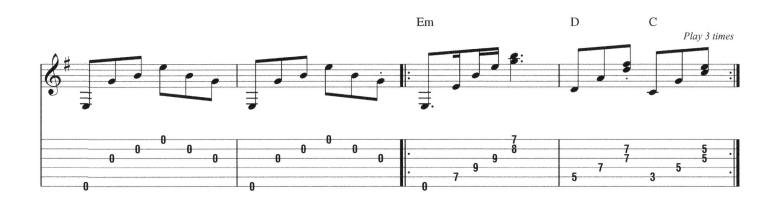

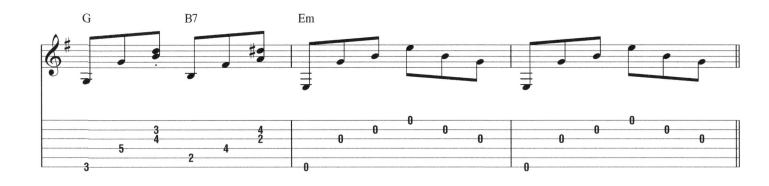

Verse

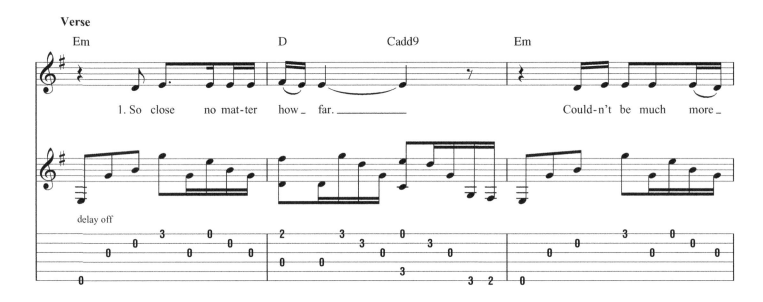

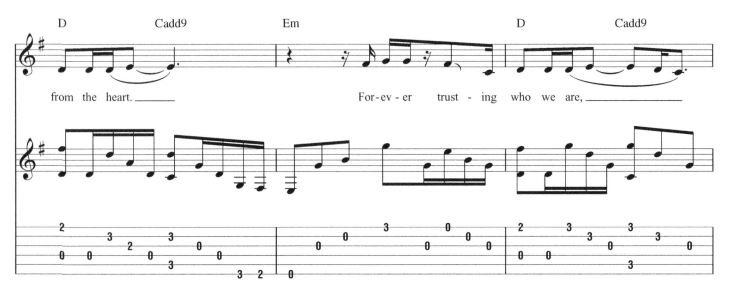

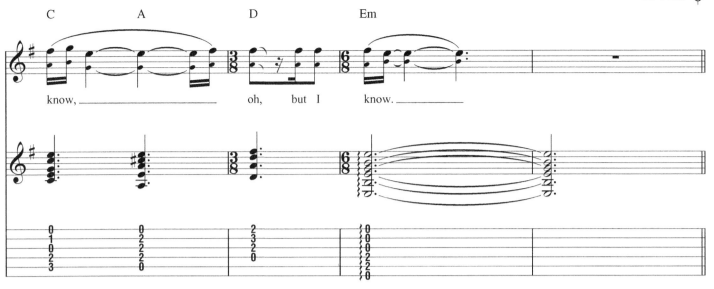

know, _____ oh, but I know.

Verse

w/ fingers

4. So close no mat-ter how _ far. _____ It could-n't be much more _

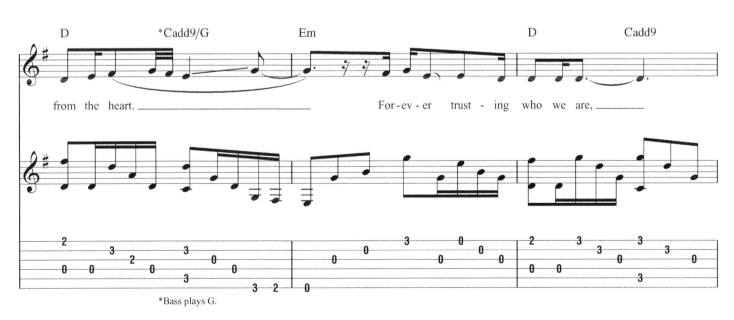

from the heart. _____ For-ev-er trust - ing who we are, _____

*Bass plays G.

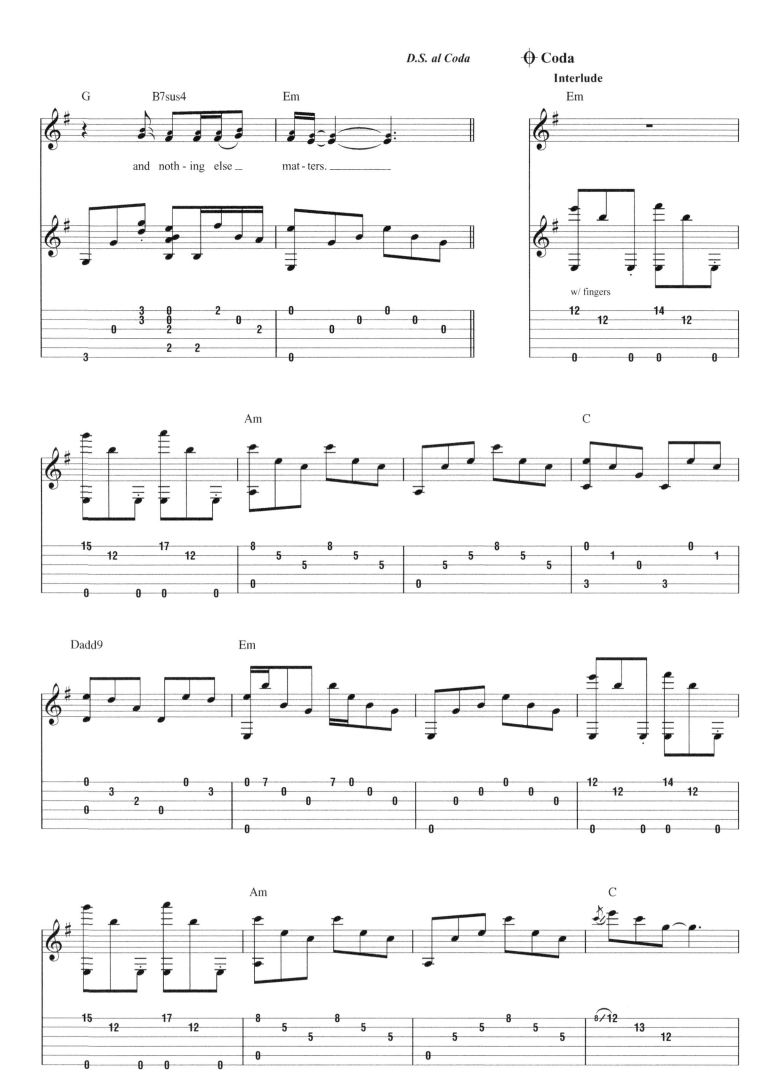

and noth - ing else _ mat - ters. _____

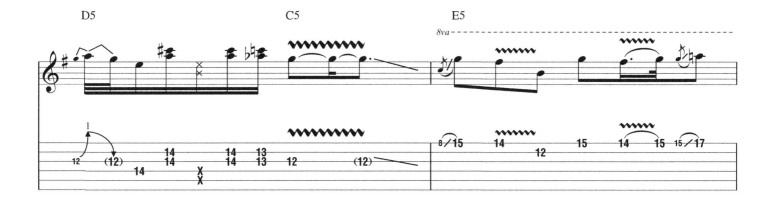

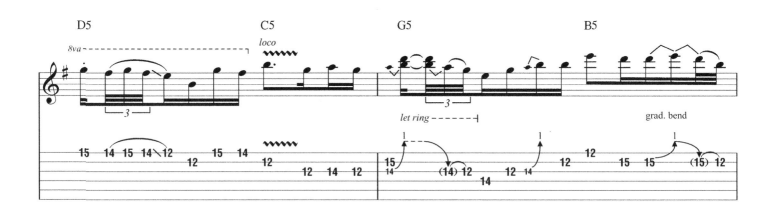

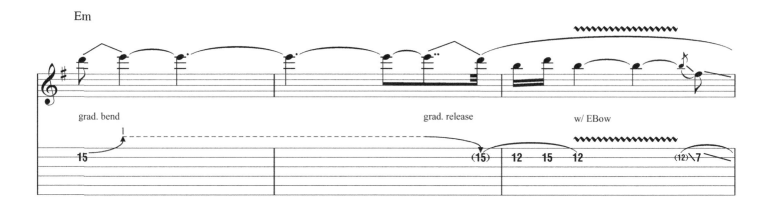

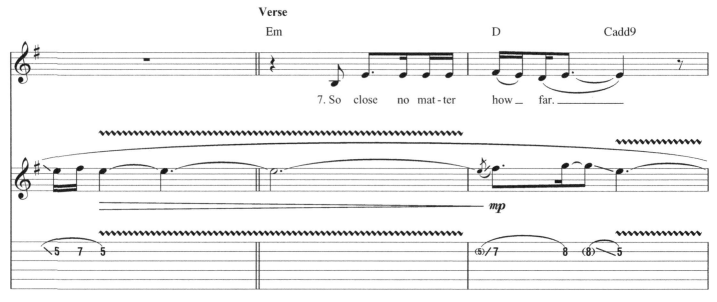

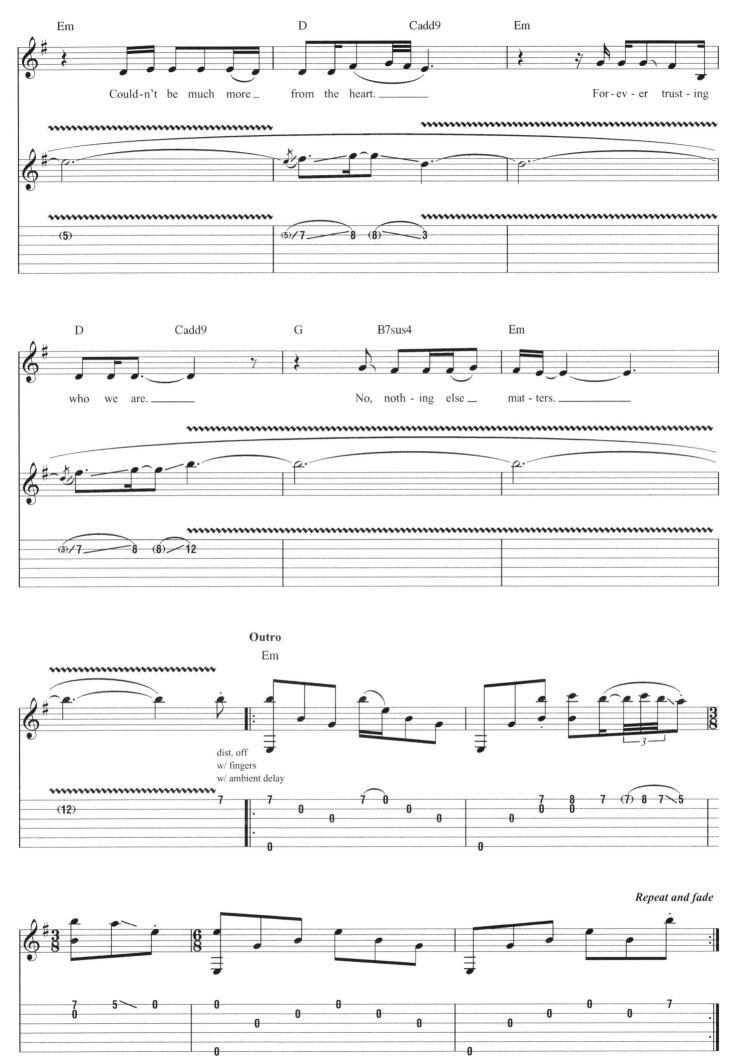

The Unforgiven

Words and Music by James Hetfield, Lars Ulrich and Kirk Hammett

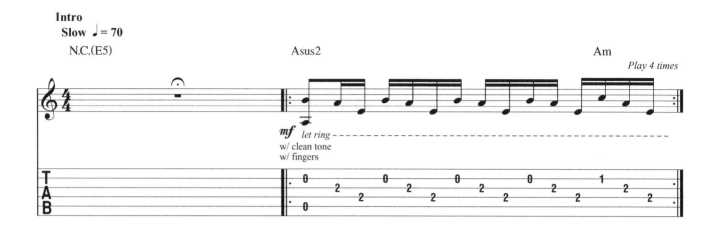

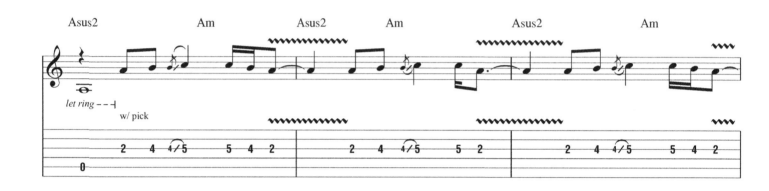

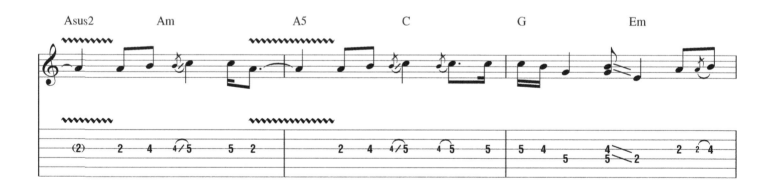

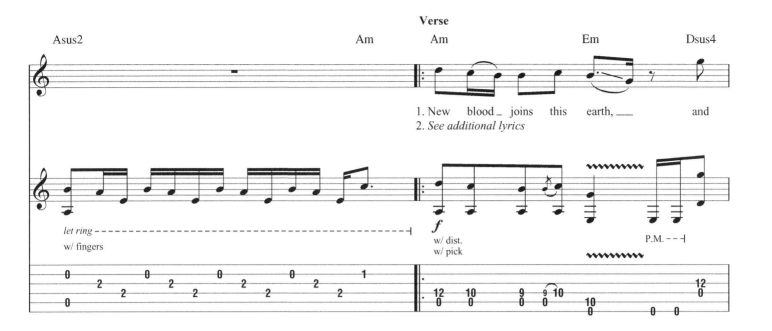

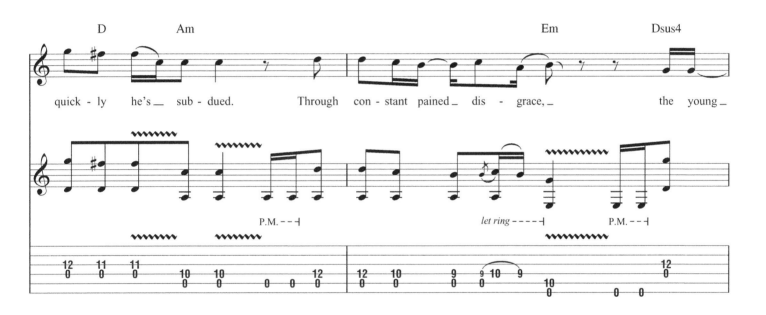

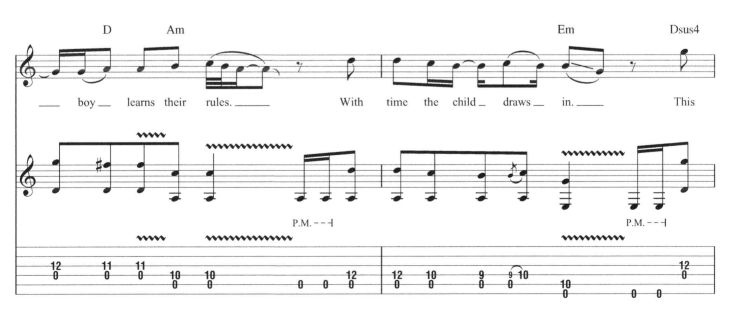

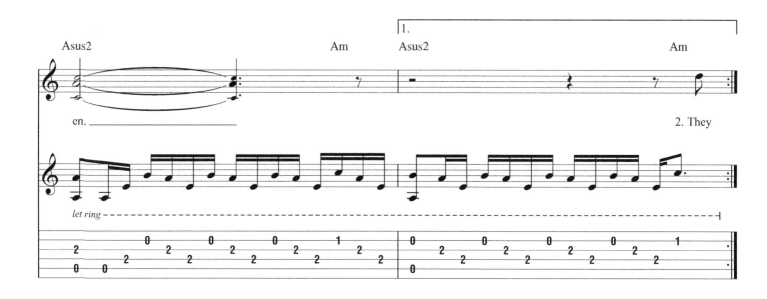

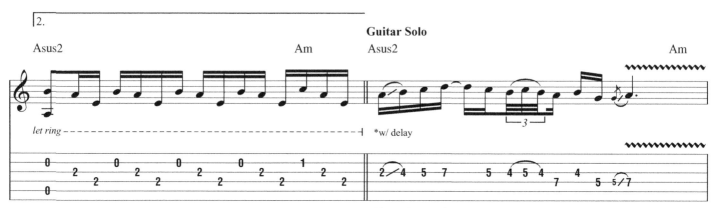

*Stereo delay set for eighth-note & quarter-note regeneration.

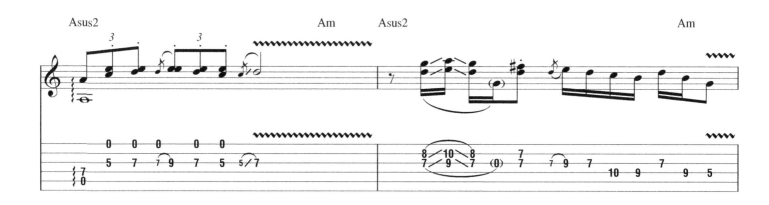

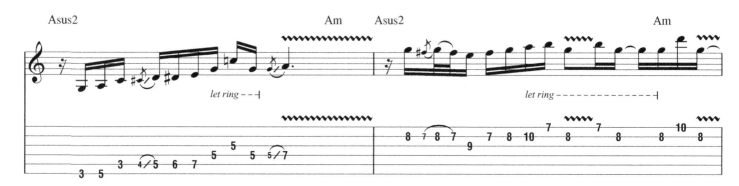

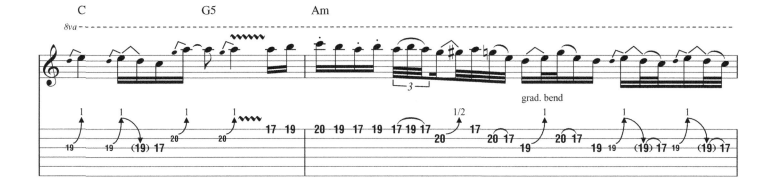

D.S. al Coda
(no repeat)

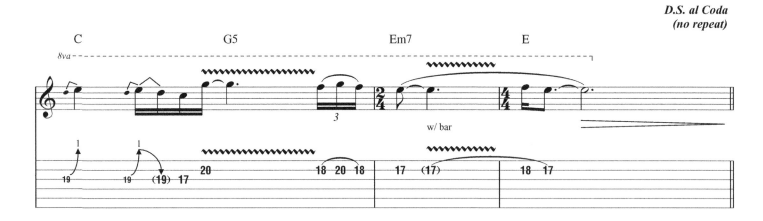

⊕ **Coda**

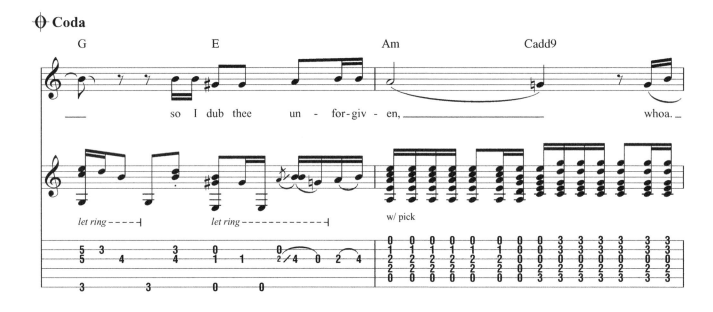

so I dub thee un-for-giv-en, _____ whoa. __

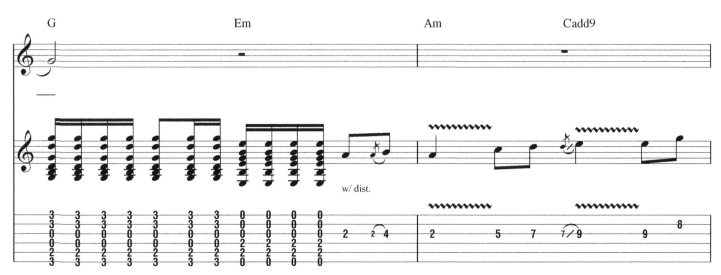

Outro-Chorus

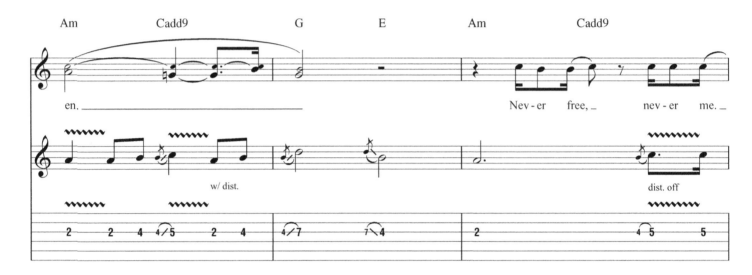

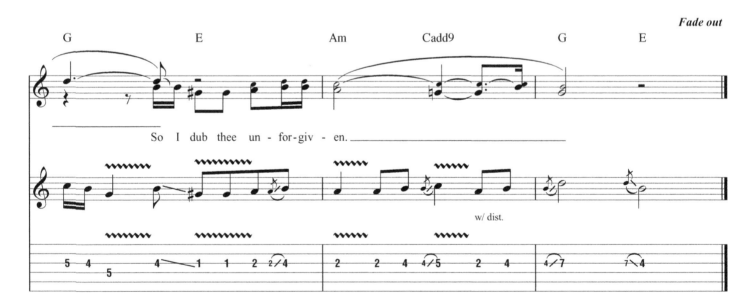

Additional Lyrics

2. They dedicate their lives to running all of his.
   He tries to please them all, this bitter man he is.
   Throughout his life the same, he's battled constantly.
   This fight he cannot win, a tired man they see no longer cares.
   The old man then prepares to die regretfully.
   That old man here is me.

HAL•LEONARD® GUITAR PLAY-ALONG

INCLUDES TAB
AUDIO ACCESS INCLUDED

This series will help you play your favorite songs quickly and easily. Just follow the tab and listen to the audio to hear how the guitar should sound, and then play along using the separate backing tracks.

Playback tools are provided for slowing down the tempo without changing pitch and looping challenging parts. The melody and lyrics are included in the book so that you can sing or simply follow along.

105. LATIN
00700939.................$16.99

106. WEEZER
00700958.................$14.99

107. CREAM
00701069.................$16.99

108. THE WHO
00701053.................$16.99

109. STEVE MILLER
00701054.................$19.99

110. SLIDE GUITAR HITS
00701055.................$16.99

111. JOHN MELLENCAMP
00701056.................$14.99

112. QUEEN
00701052.................$16.99

113. JIM CROCE
00701058.................$17.99

114. BON JOVI
00701060.................$16.99

115. JOHNNY CASH
00701070.................$16.99

116. THE VENTURES
00701124.................$17.99

117. BRAD PAISLEY
00701224.................$16.99

118. ERIC JOHNSON
00701353.................$16.99

119. AC/DC CLASSICS
00701356.................$17.99

120. PROGRESSIVE ROCK
00701457.................$14.99

121. U2
00701508.................$16.99

122. CROSBY, STILLS & NASH
00701610.................$16.99

123. LENNON & McCARTNEY ACOUSTIC
00701614.................$16.99

124. SMOOTH JAZZ
00200664.................$16.99

125. JEFF BECK
00701687.................$17.99

126. BOB MARLEY
00701701.................$17.99

127. 1970S ROCK
00701739.................$16.99

128. 1960S ROCK
00701740.................$14.99

129. MEGADETH
00701741.................$17.99

130. IRON MAIDEN
00701742.................$17.99

131. 1990S ROCK
00701743.................$14.99

132. COUNTRY ROCK
00701757.................$15.99

133. TAYLOR SWIFT
00701894.................$16.99

134. AVENGED SEVENFOLD
00701906.................$16.99

135. MINOR BLUES
00151350.................$17.99

136. GUITAR THEMES
00701922.................$14.99

137. IRISH TUNES
00701966.................$15.99

138. BLUEGRASS CLASSICS
00701967.................$17.99

139. GARY MOORE
00702370.................$16.99

140. MORE STEVIE RAY VAUGHAN
00702396.................$17.99

141. ACOUSTIC HITS
00702401.................$16.99

142. GEORGE HARRISON
00237697.................$17.99

143. SLASH
00702425.................$19.99

144. DJANGO REINHARDT
00702531.................$16.99

145. DEF LEPPARD
00702532.................$19.99

146. ROBERT JOHNSON
00702533.................$16.99

147. SIMON & GARFUNKEL
14041591.................$16.99

148. BOB DYLAN
14041592.................$16.99

149. AC/DC HITS
14041593.................$17.99

150. ZAKK WYLDE
02501717.................$19.99

151. J.S. BACH
02501730.................$16.99

152. JOE BONAMASSA
02501751.................$19.99

153. RED HOT CHILI PEPPERS
00702990.................$19.99

155. ERIC CLAPTON – FROM THE ALBUM UNPLUGGED
00703085.................$16.99

156. SLAYER
00703770.................$19.99

157. FLEETWOOD MAC
00101382.................$17.99

159. WES MONTGOMERY
00102593.................$19.99

160. T-BONE WALKER
00102641.................$17.99

161. THE EAGLES – ACOUSTIC
00102659.................$17.99

162. THE EAGLES HITS
00102667.................$17.99

163. PANTERA
00103036.................$17.99

164. VAN HALEN 1986-1995
00110270.................$17.99

165. GREEN DAY
00210343.................$17.99

166. MODERN BLUES
00700764.................$16.99

167. DREAM THEATER
00111938.................$24.99

168. KISS
00113421.................$17.99

169. TAYLOR SWIFT
00115982.................$16.99

170. THREE DAYS GRACE
00117337.................$16.99

171. JAMES BROWN
00117420.................$16.99

172. THE DOOBIE BROTHERS
00116970.................$16.99

173. TRANS-SIBERIAN ORCHESTRA
00119907.................$19.99

174. SCORPIONS
00122119.................$16.99

175. MICHAEL SCHENKER
00122127.................$17.99

176. BLUES BREAKERS WITH JOHN MAYALL & ERIC CLAPTON
00122132.................$19.99

177. ALBERT KING
00123271.................$16.99

178. JASON MRAZ
00124165.................$17.99

179. RAMONES
00127073.................$16.99

180. BRUNO MARS
00129706.................$16.99

181. JACK JOHNSON
00129854.................$16.99

182. SOUNDGARDEN
00138161.................$17.99

183. BUDDY GUY
00138240.................$17.99

184. KENNY WAYNE SHEPHERD
00138258.................$17.99

185. JOE SATRIANI
00139457.................$17.99

186. GRATEFUL DEAD
00139459.................$17.99

187. JOHN DENVER
00140839.................$17.99

188. MÖTLEY CRUE
00141145.................$17.99

189. JOHN MAYER
00144350.................$17.99

190. DEEP PURPLE
00146152.................$17.99

191. PINK FLOYD CLASSICS
00146164.................$17.99

192. JUDAS PRIEST
00151352.................$17.99

193. STEVE VAI
00156028.................$19.99

194. PEARL JAM
00157925.................$17.99

195. METALLICA: 1983-1988
00234291.................$19.99

196. METALLICA: 1991-2016
00234292.................$19.99

HAL•LEONARD®

For complete songlists, visit
Hal Leonard online at
www.halleonard.com

Prices, contents, and availability subject to
change without notice. 1120
9/12; 397